The Long Acre

Frances Corkey Thompson

Happen*Stance*

Poems © Frances Corkey Thompson, 2008
Cover image © Gillian Beaton, 2008
ISBN: 978 1 905939 25 1

Note: 'Snow-Melt' is for Chris; 'The Long Acre' is for my mother, Doreen.

Acknowledgements:
'Stonechat' was shortlisted in the Writers Inc Competition, 2007; 'Beeches at Pickwell' is drawn from a longer piece 'BirdsWords' commissioned by North Devon Arts in 2006 to accompany Emily Garnham-Wright's textile art work in Pickwell Manor Woods (www. emilygarnhamwright.co.uk/birdswords.htm).

Thanks are due to the editors of the following publications in which some of these poems first appeared: Bridport Anthology 2001; *Wherever* (Cinnamon Press Competition Anthology) 2006; *The Allotment, New Lyric Poets,* Stride, 2006; Oxford Poets 2007: An Anthology; *Irish Pages* (2003); www.lightenuponline.com; *The Rialto*; *THE SHOp.*

Printed by The Dolphin Press
www.dolphinpress.co.uk

Published in 2008 by Happen*Stance*
21 Hatton Green, Glenrothes, Fife KY7 4SD
nell@happenstancepress.com
www.happenstancepress.com

Orders:
Individual pamphlets £4.00 (including UK P&P).
Please make cheques payable to Happen*Stance* or order through PayPal on the website.

CONTENTS ✳

for

Ben and Judith

Stonechat

The stonechat is not
a stonechat. She is simply herself
on the long twig, by the stones,

no, she is not even self—it all simply
is, on this, the only possible, perfect twig.
It is *look*, and *oh!* and *flit*,

all sense and verb,
centred in the understood, measured height
of the present tense, where

giants, gravity-trapped, lumber at the edge
intoning *Territory*,
quacking *Whinchat, a related species.*

Beeches at Pickwell

Who knows them, the beeches,
with their long fingers, their long standing,
their roots that finger earth as lightly
as leaves touch air? Who in the world
has such a sense of place?

I'm not a bit curious, not a bit, not a bit
I'm not a bit curious, not a bit, not a bit

In from the west came a belt, a welter
of weather. From Pacific, Sargasso, Atlantic, Malin,
the wind ripped into the beeches, spinning
new leaves loose—leaves elliptical, feather-veined, spatulate.
The moth cowered, confounded, and the owl, and the grub
in the old man's beard. Rain blew in, to bathe
the last primrose, to bless sorrel, drench mosses,
paint lichens, oil the wheels of ferns, sluice bark,
usher in bluebells, nettles and docks, and prime
dandelions' soft time-bombs.

Pippa-chee! Chirrup! Tripper-tea! Tripper-tea for two!

Air was glass. Trees
hardly dared to breathe. The buzzard hung high,
the hare and the shrew
                                        hid.

The heart thudded. A thorn? —a big bad wolf?
—the witch in her gingerbread house? —a man
green and not moving a tendril, though wooed
by churches and midges?
Can't see the wood for the trees
are too near. Can't see the wood for fear,
for a bird, whose hush-hush name is Fear...

Have you been to the doctor? have you been to the ...
Have you been to the doctor? have you been to the ...

A long finger lifts a fern,
weighs, drops, lifts it again ...

Snow-Melt

The ache of it spiralled from head to bones.
It was late afternoon, late summer,
and I looked at the stream's steep walls
and saw the difficulty, the inadvisability,
the impossibility of going down there.

As I stood to walk on, I saw above me
all the crowds of pines yielding steam like horses
and clouds ballooning white on blue. The globe
of the world was a creature breathing,
and under the bridge

the grey-green water, running.
A small bird shot from her place in the bank
and I kicked off my shoes and my plain
bare warm animal feet took me down into
what I could not have imagined.

Owl

Owl is heavy, says
you can't write such
things, don't write that,
knows too much.

Owl sits on my shoulder.
Sits there fifty years. Woooo!
Says I was there so I know
better than you.

Owl is fading.
Grow thin, Owl, grow light.
Blow away to Owl-Heaven.
Blow away tonight.

Kernel

Unable to sleep, I make
downstairs for the fridge,
neck some milk and outside
the kitchen window it's bright
with rain and streetlights.
A stripe of light paints the landing—

a stage.

My bed is luminous
and in the next room my daughter
breathes and waits as the child held in her
also waits. Yesterday
she said, *Some things will go on
the same, Mum, won't they?*

Fiat Deus ...

... for the green plastic watering-can,
for the tilted chairs, for water
guttering over grass and stone—
for the moment of rain in the garden.

Somewhere out there is the frog
whose perfect burping punctuated our talk.
Surely there was a god for the frog that day
and for the way we laughed? Surely

there is a god for the rain loading
my watering-can green and large as itself
filling my window let there at least
be a god for this god-awful

hammering rain.
Green watering-can on sodden garden furniture.
Invisible frog. My visible
breath on the window.

The Garden

It draws you, the place, although
it is often raining and I have often chosen
to stand, barefoot

on this slab or on that slab
and I have even tried, in stupid hope,
to balance on both at the same time

but I was young then. Now
that the blades of my shoulders have settled
free of my neck, I get the point

of rods and clusters thrusting
under their own steam
and the birch dripping in its green weight

and how the banners of untethered honeysuckle
flip and toss their challenge. No longer
part of the action, I witness through glass

the snail on the attack and the
jasmine hooking up with the rose
and the rosemary that was always in blue bloom

dying. For a moment I am beak to beak
with a sparrow at my window.
It drops its white bead and is gone, alerted

to the dark, living shadow.

Mrs Jones

These walls hold the business of the house—
they are marked by the red fingers of maids

who cut root vegetables, who kneel, at dawn,
at fireplaces. Listen

for the hollow slop of water-jugs carried up
or chamberpots brought, at armslength, down

my long stairs, or the snap and chuckle
of a banister, where warm bodies might lean.

Mrs Jones lived here for ninety years
and moved on long ago. Now she is back

giving orders for a new look for the walls.
She has chosen a hand-painted paper

with leaves that twine and hide,
brown and black when I uncover them,

hints of skin on the air today, of breath
catching my own breath, blood on the tongue.

It is never quiet, this house of mine. Mrs Jones
has taken a lamp down to the cellar. She moves

the surf-boards aside, to check on her preserves,
her jellies in jars, their low fires.

The Boy Who Understands Light

His forehead is white in his moon-face.
He stares through light
listening for the music of dust.
He shares sundowns with the cows
in the field below the lighthouse.

He ignores mirrors—
they are too cold for his skinny arms
and beyond his reach. He treads softly
because floor is loose and airy as sunbeams.
A struck match is a dance

as ecstatic, as dangerous as glass.
He is a crow flapping on a black sky
above a street teeming with life
and all its chairs and tables occupied
and all its lamps ablaze.

Tommy Not There

When they explained to us
that Tommy was dead and gone

we ran to his hutch, to see
Tommy not there

and kept returning, to inspect
his straw for scuffle, his scraps

of dead lettuce for nibble,
and coming again until

tickled noses and warm flop-ears
settled as memory, and we could see

Tommy-not-there
so clearly, that the hutch

freed itself of Tommy and slipped
into its new, empty status.

As Tommy entered eternity, we left it.
We had thoughts to suck on

like big boiled sweets.

Lough Neagh

I

They could read water, the Lough people—
a pool of light, a ruffle. The Lough,
chill as a human shiver, told of trout or eel,
of rain, of the tight line between hunger and enough,
between sex and dying.

In the long evenings, companionship
could be felt on the flats of the hand,
could be breathed, a narcotic that drove
human greed, need and flow, fitting
like a glove around the brain, explaining it all

except for the puzzle-pictures
where a beetle might bark like a dog
or a human child fade in the sun, though fed,
and be folded, with her treasures,
into the dark under bright mosses.

Through nights, through short, dangerous days
the fire centred them, the Lough people,
drew their minds, blackened faces. They knew
how to surfeit and celebrate, when to die.
The woman, dulled with damage, survived

into the time of thickening leaves and birds' clamour
when tree and cloud lay clean on the Lough's face
and the midges multiplied to a haze in its bushy inlets.
Then she would creep and stoop
to place the wild anemones that love the shade

above her child, and sing to it,
though it not hearing. She gave it her secret name.
She came to the place from the Lough.
She came in the morning, her long hair flashing,
her body white.

II

Like some forgotten foundling ghost
the white-bodied woman stoops and creeps
stirring my settled waters.

I am stalked in the dark by stories—
not of flawed Achillean heroes, or unicorns,
or people of dreams—

She is of herself, trailing ash and verdigris,
moving in poppy, heliotrope, verbena
and wind-blown marigold.

She will not rest.
I will not invite her to rest,
to stir tea in a cup.

She knows the codling moth and the comma
and the milkweed, and the small dimpling hand
that my mother knows.

I turn from her—we have no common talk.
When I look, she has slipped
back to the water.

III

In a bedlam of birds and breezes
I found a flat stone by the Lough.

My hands went in, refracted,
paling, and my arms to the elbow.

The hospital windows flashed
but the Lough was blind, and gathered

thick-flecked, on me,
building a causeway to the sky,

to yet more Ireland. My hands
were fins, working as if a creature

could outwit water, as if will
could reorder the world.

The Disgruntled Lover

That you would turn me down, I never dreamt.
I was nonplussed that you would choose a youth
so rough and rude, in aspect so unkempt,
in manner so decidedly uncouth.

Disgruntled and distressed, in short I wept.
With fierce hot tears my eiderdown I scorched,
lamenting what had happened. How inept
to lose my love to one who was debauched!

At length my cries abated. Then, dishevelled,
my face a mess, my hair (like his) unruly,
I made myself a meal of kidneys (devilled)
and wondered if I'd ever loved you truly.

Now tressed and hevelled, once more kempt, in truth
I'm gruntled, bauched, plussed, ruly, ept and couth.

Wanting to Run on Grass

After a few days in the sandy house
with sandy children by a sandy beach
Ben, who was four, said
that he wanted to run on grass

but there was no grass—only sand
and road. Then we remembered
a grassy place near the gates of St Malo.
Because it was Ben's holiday too

we left Judith with the French family
and went. The grass was a mile or two away.
For the last part of our journey
Ben rode piggy-back.

When we reached the grass I set him down
and he ran and ran and ran. He ran
until he was a distant, blue-and-red scamper.
Then he ran back. Then off again.

Grass, being half-rooted and half-free
is better for running on than sand. Grass
grounds the foot. At lift-off, each shoot
lends its own thrust.

Woodpigeons in France

Our parlance
soft pulses of woodwind,

our notes nouns
honed to a euphony,

our declensions
a gentle hullabaloo.

Only our inflections waver,
how we colour our tones—

our crooning moving, always,
to the hanging, verbless question

that pipes, unanswered,
again and again through the still afternoon,

our small, baffled cadences ebbing
        too soon ...

The Long Acre

Johnny Gilcreesh
grazes his three goats
out on the Long Acre

moves the tethers on
a yard or so
every day or so,

picks and chooses
primrose-banks in season,
violet and vetch

avoids dock, yew
blown across
from the graveyard.

Then the motorbike.
Fellow broke his leg. Goat
didn't feel a thing.

While the police measured
and asked questions
Johnny Gilcreesh

lay low with his two goats.
Now they are out again
on the Long Acre.

Lush, the Long Acre.
Lovely milk
and bothering no farmer.

Silence at the Big Top

Trapeze artists do not defy gravity so much as use it.
In their mingled flights, hands seek and grip—
they work their swift machine, and soar
till her small feet alight on a high landing—
and he's off again, an aerial postman
delivering more miracles for the crowd

until the day she flew, no safety-net
and he, happening, for a split second,
to be distracted by his own reflection
in a thousand wondering eyes below,
missed contact. There's more than one way
to let a person down.

She knew it, the splitting second before it happened
or didn't happen. She still described a perfect arc,
only now outward and down—
graceful as a glittering swallow, empty hands wide
and eyes wide, and the world
had never been so wonderful

as it was then. There were the upturned faces
and the fixed eyes, still wondering,
and the glint of sun on the grass at the tent-flaps
and the silence
as if the band had stopped playing.
Yes. The silence.

So now fill this silence with beautiful flying things—
with creatures that live and die in a day. Let there be
a flurry of flapping, whirring, buzzing,
bumbling in the summer grasses of bees,
zing of beetles with lapis lazuli wings, dragons,
eagles tilting to the sun.

Looking for My Mother in Marks & Spencer
and Finding Her

I am looking for my mother in Marks & Spencer.
We came in to see what they had in skirts. It has to be
light, a sensible colour, comfortable at the waist
and most importantly, it must have pockets. She tries on.
I go in search again, and advise.

Now I have lost her. We took a break from skirts,
were casually hunting in blouses just in case,
then she was gone. Round the other side of the rack, maybe.
Two small, smart pastel ladies are chatting there,
neither of them my mother.

She can scuttle along the street so quickly.
When she turned eighty, she felt she was slowing down.
Thank goodness, I said, *give me a chance to keep up.*
But I still can't. She could be anywhere in the shop by now.
Where should I start?

She might have taken a fancy to checking the upper floor.
For minutes, I stare at the escalators. White heads
are flowing up, floating down, cotton-wool clouds
on God's production lines. All of them could be,
not one of them is, my mother.

I start looking in earnest. There are three of her
ferreting in Summer Dresses. Two are fingering Men's Socks,
six dallying in Lingerie, and a horde heading for the Food Hall.
How many short ladies in pale turquoise jackets
can there be in the world?

Here she is coming towards me. Crowds block the way.
A split second, but you always know your mother's face—
a little desolate now, a little lost with looking.
The people part, and I am smiling, stupidly, at myself
in a Marks & Spencer's mirror ...

as my mother finds me, touches my arm. *There you are!*
What do you think of this one? She is holding up
a skirt that looks just perfect. It will go with her silk top.
It will be beautiful with her turquoise jacket.
It has good pockets.

Pouring Tea

This is how tea is poured now.
This is how we offer, accept, eat, drink,
do with our hands what hands do.

Let us turn our faces from the fact
that we need no sugar-bowl today.
Have you ever known a room to be so full?

Side by side on the edges of sofas
we brim with him. We have thrown
a safe green belt around his name.

When grubs turn to moths and slip
from earth to sky, how do they perceive
gravity's shift? Let us warmly greet

the person who comes with forms to fill.
Let our fingers close on the pen she offers.
Let the pen spill itself into the right boxes

and let her papers be folded with care. So this
is how *widow* is pronounced, and this
is how steam rises when tea is poured.

This is how the lip is burned
at the first sip.

The Safe Places

They are places of danger,
all of them. Even here
on the homeward path where the road forks

making a triangle out of Nowhere
you could be lured by tall unkindly irises
to fall and drown.

In the woods where bluebells
hide the beetle and the hedgehog
we stand by the mouse-grey stream

where they have put up barbed wire
so that even here it is safe no longer.
Turn. Look on the wrong side.

The safest place is not where I said.
The child knew and she has kept the secret.
One day I will find you.

Ur

After the first, there is no other.
It was like watching a good film in Czech
or standing in an overheated gallery

before a Dali painting—the back of you
making for vanishing point, trees and leaves
whipping you along a pavement

that curled itself into a Boston sky.
The moment of it I didn't get for months.
Abraham probably stepped out of Ur

with the same sort of stride—
though with more company—not looking back
as you did not look back

not risking that last sight of a girl
in a newly-Authorised Version of October wind,
her own personal translation,

and fending off already
her mother's *What on earth's the matter dear?*—
the helpless hang of the Boys' Brigade tea-towel.

Severance

The man who is splitting stones
says that the rock,
in the moment before it breaks,
speaks—
gives a leathery *Yes*
along its agreed lines
of surrender.

I think of how,
when you slice a carrot
lengthways,
it springs apart from itself
as if it has been waiting
all of its life
for this relief.

Sometimes, says the man,
you get smooth stone,
that doesn't so much crack
as slide apart
in great curved slabs.
I see cooked codflesh,
gleaming.

He feels
he is granting a favour
to the damp virgin rock-face
that has not yet
been frosted with dew
or salted, or crusted
with lichen.

The Old Woman Wishes for a Road

Make me a road I can walk once more—
a road with white houses, on a white shore

and there must be sand, banked well
and scattered, ground out of shell

out of bone, out of stone in the sea's eye—
a road under rain, and a wind to dry.

Then I'll hitch up my skirts and I'll run, shouting—
I'll run with the children, shouting, shouting.